Druid was founded in Galway in 1975 by graduates of the National University of Ireland, Galway – Garry Hynes, Marie Mullen and Mick Lally. The company has had two artistic directors; Garry Hynes (1975–91 and 1995 to date) and Maeliosa Stafford (1991–94).

Druid aims to create electrifying theatre experiences for every person, in every place and every time they perform. The company presents work at home in Galway and tours extensively in Ireland. Druid also tours to key global centres around the world making it one of the premier theatre companies in the English-speaking world.

Recent productions include *The Gigli Concert* by Tom Murphy, *The Cripple of Inishmaan* by Martin McDonagh (winner of nine US, UK and Irish theatre awards), *The New Electric Ballroom* by Enda Walsh (Edinburgh Fringe First Winner, 2008; Irish Times Best New Play Award, 2009) and *The Walworth Farce* by Enda Walsh (Edinburgh Fringe First Winner, 2007). Druid's world premiere of Martin McDonagh's *The Beauty Queen of Leenane* (1996) went on to win four Tony Awards in 1998, including Best Director for Garry Hynes.

Druid's previous partnerships with Enda Walsh (*The Walworth Farce*, *The New Electric Ballroom*) have led to sell-out runs in six countries worldwide, wowing critics and audiences alike.

For more information about Druid see www.druid.ie

STAY IN TOUCH
For up-to-date news on Druid, please visit our website www.druid.ie and join our mailing list.

SUPPORTING DRUID
If you would like to support the ongoing work of Druid, please contact us at giving@druid.ie or on +353 91 568 660.

Acknowledgements
Druid acknowledges and is grateful for the financial support of the Arts Council for funding the original staging of our shows, and to Culture Ireland for funding our international touring programme.

Druid wishes to express its continuing gratitude to Thomas McDonagh & Company Ltd for their support of the company and gratefully acknowledges the assistance of Galway City Council and Galway County Council.

Druid

Druid presents

PENELOPE
By ENDA WALSH

**8 – 24 JULY 2010 DRUID LANE THEATRE, GALWAY
AS PART OF GALWAY ARTS FESTIVAL**

27 – 31 JULY 2010 EVERYMAN PALACE THEATRE, CORK

**5 – 29 AUGUST 2010 TRAVERSE THEATRE, EDINBURGH
AS PART OF EDINBURGH FESTIVAL FRINGE**

**1 – 2 SEPTEMBER 2010 KORJAAMO CULTURE FACTORY,
HELSINKI AS PART OF STAGE FESTIVAL 2010, FINLAND**

9 – 12 SEPTEMBER 2010 TOWN HALL THEATRE, GALWAY

**14 – 18 SEPTEMBER 2010 PAVILION THEATRE,
DÚN LAOGHAIRE, CO. DUBLIN**

Penelope received its premiere at Theater Oberhausen, Germany on 27 February
2010. Druid presented the English-language premiere in Druid Lane Theatre at the
Galway Arts Festival on 13 July, 2010

PENELOPE
By ENDA WALSH

FITZ	**Niall Buggy**
DUNNE	**Denis Conway**
BURNS	**Tadhg Murphy**
QUINN	**Karl Shiels**
PENELOPE	**Olga Wehrly**

DIRECTOR	**Mikel Murfi**
DESIGNER	**Sabine Dargent**
LIGHTING DESIGNER	**Paul Keogan**
SOUND DESIGNER	**Gregory Clarke**
CASTING DIRECTOR	**Maureen Hughes**

Production Manager	Eamonn Fox
Company Stage Manager	Sarah Lynch
Stage Director	Lee Davis
Assistant Stage Manager (Galway)	Danny Erskine
Assistant Stage Manager (Tour)	Rachel Godding
Technical Manager	Barry O'Brien
Set Construction	Gus Dewar, Tony Cording
Costume Supervisor	Doreen McKenna
Wardrobe Mistress (Galway)	Amanda Donovan
Wardrobe Mistress (Tour)	Sarah Holland
Scenic Artist	Sandra Butler
Wigs and Make-up	Val Sherlock
Lighting Technicians	Shannon Light, Pat O'Reilly
Crew	Peter Nelson, Mick McLoughney, Tim Byrne, Keith Newman, Noel Tate, Jason McCafferty
Magic Consultants	Keelan Leyser, Charlotte Marie
Special Effects	Black Powder Monkeys
Props	Matt Guinane
Transport	Trevor Price
Publicist	Kate Bowe PR, Cliona Roberts CRPR
Graphic Design	Bite! Associates
Production Photography	Robert Day
Cover Image Photographer	Sarah Jones

Additional Thanks

Druid gratefully acknowledges the assistance and support of the many people who helped with this production including Sé Purcell, Blacklight, Alex Fernie, Paul Fahy and John Crumlish at Galway Arts Festival, Oddie Sherwin, Bryan Dunne, Michael Slattery & Associates, Syl Harty, East Galway Fire Prevention, Galway Fire Service, Pat O'Grady, Mongey Communications, Pan Pan Theatre, Rynn Engineering, Deirdre Looney, Aine Caulfield and all those who have helped with the production of *Penelope* since this publication went to print.

CAST

NIALL BUGGY *Fitz*

Druid: *Gentrification* (Enda Walsh one-act play, 2008).

Other theatre includes: *Haunted* (Manchester Royal Exchange); *After Play, Uncle Vanya* (Gate Theatre, Dublin); *Translations* (Broadway, MTC); *A Kind of Alaska, A Slight Ache* (Gate Theatre, London); *Guys and Dolls* (Donmar); *The Gigli Concert* (Finborough Theatre); *John Bull's Other Island* (Tricycle Theatre); *Mr Nobody* (Soho Theatre); *An Inspector Calls* (Playhouse Theatre); *The Weir* (Duke of York's, Broadway and Sydney); *Give Me Your Answer Do, Song at Sunset* (Hampstead Theatre); *Dead Funny* (Hampstead Theatre and Vaudeville); *Aristocrats* (Hampstead Theatre and New York); *The Misanthrope* (Young Vic); *Juno and the Paycock* (Albery Theatre); *Drama at Inish, The Cherry Orchard, The Seagull* (Abbey Theatre, Dublin); *The Rivals, Rough Crossing, Love for Love, Threepenny Opera* (National Theatre); *The School for Scandal, Hamlet, Arms and the Man* (Haymarket, Leicester); *Travesties* (Liverpool Playhouse); *Memoir* (Ambassador Theatre); *Blood Knot, The Actress and the Bishop* (King's Head); *Spokesong* (Vaudeville); *The Shadow of a Gunman, Dwarfs* (Young Vic); *The Birthday Party, Waiting for Godot* (Crucible Theatre); *John Bull* (Bristol Old Vic); *One of Our Own* (Gaiety Theatre, Dublin); *The Three Sisters* (Field Day Theatre); *Kill* (Sleehun Theatre, Dublin); *Shadow of a Gunman* (Irish tour and USA).

Film & Television: *The Duel, Mamma Mia!, Casanova, The Libertine, Spin the Bottle, Morality Play, Anna Karenina, Sweeney Todd, The Butcher Boy, The Lonely Passion of Judith Hearne* (Handmade Films); *Hellraiser, Close My Eyes, The Playboys, King David* (Paramount Pictures); *Philadelphia Here I Come, Portrait of the Artist as a Young Man, Zaz Doz, Sleeping with the Fishes, Aliens III, Dental Breakdown* (Rocket Productions); *Malice Aforethought* (ITV); *Grease Monkeys, Agony Too, Full Wax, The Hummingbird Tree, Once in a Lifetime, Galloping Galaxies, The Gathering Seed, The Citadel, Nanny, Red Roses for Me, Chinese Whispers* (BBC), *The Cruise, Family Affairs, Lucy Sullivan is Getting* (Carnival Films); *Married, Upwardly Mobile* (STE); *Father Ted* (Channel 4), *Little Napoleons* (Picture Palace), *99 to 1* (Zenith), *Fair City, The Famine, The Farmers, The Promise* (RTÉ); *Chancer* (Central TV), *The Bill, The Professionals* (ITV); *The Little Mother* (Granada), *The Sleeping Life* (TVS).

Awards: Niall is the recipient of a number of awards including Best Actor Award, Irish Times Irish Theatre Awards, *Uncle Vanya*; Olivier Award, *Dead Funny*; Best Actor, Regional Theatre Award, *Juno and the Paycock*; Time Out Award, Obie Award, Drama Desk Award, Clarence Derwent Award for his role as Casimir in *Aristocrats*; a Harvey Award for *The Three Sisters*; Helen Haynes Nomination for *Shadow of a Gunman*.

DENIS CONWAY *Dunne*

Druid: *The Gigli Concert* (Galway and Irish tour); *The Walworth Farce* (National Theatre, London and New York, 2008; Edinburgh Fringe Festival, 2007; Galway, Cork and Dublin, 2006); *The Playboy of the Western World* (Perth, Australia tour 2005).

Other theatre includes: *Christ Deliver Us, The Recruiting Officer, Homeland, A Cry from Heaven, The Dandy Dolls, Riders to the Sea, The Wild Duck, Freedom of the City, The Colleen Bawn, April Bright, The Crucible, The Comedy of Errors* (Abbey and Peacock Theatres); *Wallenstein* (Chichester Festival Theatre); *The Death of Harry Leon, Making History* (tour to commemorate the 400th anniversary of *The Flight of the Earls*); *Myrmidons, Amadeus, Macbeth, Tales from Ovid, Richard III, Mutabilitie, Troilus and Cressida* (Ouroboros Theatre Co.); *Diarmuid and Gráinne, Studs, Native City, Buddleia* (Passion Machine); *Volpone, Castle Rackrent, Miss Julie, The Overcoat, Lear* (Meridian); *Conversations on a Homecoming, Una Pooka, One for the Road* (Feedback).

Film & Television: *Zonad* (dirs John and Ciarán Kearney); *Garage* (dir. Lenny Abrahamson); *Tiger's Tail* (dir. John Boorman); *The Wind that Shakes the Barley* (dir. Ken Loach); *Boy Eats Girl* (dir. Stephen Bradley); *Alexander* (dir. Oliver Stone); *Yesterday's Children* (dir. Marcus Cole); *Intermission* (dir. John Crowley); *The Borstal Boy* (dir. Peter Sheridan); *The Countess Cathleen* (dir. Paula Bergin); *I Went Down* (dir. Paddy Breathnach); *Michael Collins* (dir. Neil Jordan); *Making Ends Meet* (dir. Declan Recks); *Single Handed, Hide and Seek, Showbands 1 and 2, The Clinic, Bachelors Walk, On Home Ground, Fair City* (RTÉ); *Rebel Heart, Casualty, Custer's Last Stand Up, Ballykissangel* (BBC); *Yesterday's Children* (CBS); *Running Mate, Trí Scéal, Boghaisíní* (TG4).

Awards: Denis was awarded the Best Actor Award at the Irish Times Irish Theatre Awards (2009) for his role as The Irishman in the Druid production of *The Gigli Concert* by Tom Murphy. In 2001 he also won the Best Actor award for his role as Richard in Ouroboros Theatre Company's production of *Richard III*. In 2008, he was nominated in the category of Best Actor for his role as Vincent in *Running Mate* in the Irish Film and Television Awards (IFTA).

Denis is Artistic Director of Ouroboros Theatre Company.

TADHG MURPHY *Burns*

Tadhg trained at the Samuel Beckett Centre, Trinity College Dublin with a Bachelor in Acting Studies.

Druid: *The Walworth Farce* (World Tour – Ireland, UK, Canada, USA, Australia, New Zealand 2009–2010; National Theatre, London, New York, Galway, Dublin, 2008; Edinburgh Festival Fringe, 2007); *Empress of India* (Galway and Dublin Theatre Festival).

Other theatre: *MedEia* (Corcodorca); *Three Sisters, Julius Caesar, The Importance of Being Earnest, Harold and Sophie* (Abbey Theatre); *Alice in Wonderland, The Goat* (Landmark Productions); *Dublin by Lamplight* (Corn Exchange); *Drive By* (Performance Corporation); *The Taming of the Shrew* (Rough Magic); *Titus Andronicus* (Siren Productions); *Shooting Gallery* (Bedrock Theatre Co.); *Deathtrap* (Red Kettle); *The Real Thing* (Gúna Nua Theatre Co.); *Fando and Lis* (Project); *Macbeth, Romeo and Juliet* (Second Age Theatre Co.); *The Real Thing, A Christmas Carol* (Gate Theatre, Dublin); *The Divorcement of Figaro, Triumph of Love, New Morning* (Samuel Beckett Centre); *Oedipus* (Players Theatre, TCD).

Film & Television: *The Clinic, Pride and Joy* (ARC Productions); *Jelly Baby* (Manifesto); *Boy Eats Girl* (Sitric Films); *Alexander* (Intermedial); *Good Man Danny* (DIT); *Hide and Seek* (RTÉ/Accomplice Films); *Love is the Drug* (RTÉ/West Street Films); *No Tears* (One Films).

Radio: numerous plays for RTÉ Radio, including *The Plough and the Stars, The Finnegans, The Colleen and the Cowboy.*

Tadhg received a nomination for Best Supporting Actor for the feature film, *Boy Eats Girl*, at the 2005 Irish Film and Television Awards.

KARL SHIELS *Quinn*

Druid: *Penelope* marks Karl's debut with Druid.

Other theatre includes: *Macbeth, Terminus, The Comedy of Errors, The Resistible Rise of Arturo Ui, Romeo and Juliet, Beauty in a Broken Place, Henry IV Part I, Barbaric Comedies, At Swim-Two-Birds, Twenty Grand* (Abbey Theatre); *The Death of Harry Leon* (Ouroboros Theatre); *Hue and Cry* (Bewleys Café, Oran Mor, Glasgow); *The Pride of Parnell Street* (Fishamble/International tour); *Howie the Rookie* (international tour); *Oedipus Loves You* (international tour); *Sleeping Beauty* (Helix); *The Shadow of a Gunman* (Lyric Theatre, Belfast); *Duck* (Royal Court); *Salomé* (Gate Theatre, Dublin); *Greek, Quartet, Muller's Medea, Obituary, Early Morning, This Lime Tree Bower, The Massacre @ Paris, Fully Recovered, The Spanish Tragedy, The Duchess of Malfi* (Project Arts Centre); *Hamlet, Venus and Adonis* (Samuel Beckett Centre); *Comedians* (Dublin Theatre Festival).

As a Director: Karl is Artistic Director of Semper Fi (Ireland) where he directed *Adrenalin, God's Grace, Ladies and Gents, Ten, Slaughter, Breakfast with Versace, Within 24 Hours, Another 24 Hours, Within 24 Hours of Dance, Conversation with a Cupboard Man, Butterflies, Black Bessie.* He has also directed *The Dark Room* (Gentle Giant); *Topdog/Underdog, Three Tall Women* (Tall Tales); *Drapes, Eggshell, Bernard Opens Up* (Fishamble); *Gargarin Way* (Island); *The Pitchfork Disney, Fallen* (Raw Image).

Film & Television: *Trafficked, Prejudice, Knockout, Butchers, No Justice, At Death's Door, Savage, Eden, W.C., Prosperity, Batman Begins, Intermission, Spin the Bottle, Get Rich or Die Tryin', Veronica Guerin, Mystics, Clubbing, Freaky Deaky 10/1, Meeting Che Guevera and the Man from Maybury Hill, Daybreak, Capital Letters* (Best Actor Irish Film and Television Award nomination, 2002), *The Tudors, Doctors, Attachments, Getting Close, Waiting for Dublin, Virtues of a Sinner, The Anarchic Hand Affair, The Clinic, Private Lives, Any Time Now, On Home Ground, Camera Café.*

Awards: Nominated for a Best Supporting Actor Award, Irish Times Irish Theatre Awards, for his role as Tommy Stein in *The Death of Harry Leon* (Smock Alley); Best Actor Award, *Comedians* (Dublin Theatre Festival, 1999).

OLGA WEHRLY *Penelope*

Druid: *Penelope* marks Olga's debut with Druid.

Other theatre: *Helter Skelter, Red Light Winter* (Purple Heart Theatre Company); *All of Human Life is Here* (Volta Productions, Dublin Fringe Festival 2009); *Macbeth, Othello* (Second Age); *Whereabouts – Drapes, Blind Spot* (Fishamble); *Wuthering Heights* (City Theatre Dublin); *Sexual Perversity in Chicago* (Icarus Theatre).

Film & Television: *Blood Coloured Moon* (Cleverality Pictures); *The Crush* (Purdy Pictures); *Rásaí na Gaillimhe/The Galway Races* (TG4); *The Clinic, Raw, This is Nightlive* (RTÉ); *Ape* (Channel 4); *Nuts* (Media Factory); *One Christmas Eve* (Christmas Eve Productions); *The Alarms* (Caboom); *Speed Dating* (System 48); *Foireann Codladh/TEAM SLEEP* (Newgrange Pictures); *Life Drawing* (Cutstone Films); *Uri's Haunted Venice* (BSkyB).

CREATIVE TEAM

ENDA WALSH Writer

Druid: *The New Electric Ballroom* (Obie Award, 2010; Edinburgh Fringe First Award, 2008; Best New Play, Irish Times Theatre Awards, 2008); *The Walworth Farce* (Edinburgh Fringe First Award, 2007); one-act plays *Lynndie's Gotta Gun* and *Gentrification*.

Other theatre: *Delirium*, an adaptation of Dostoevsky's *The Brothers Karamazov* (for Theatre O, Abbey Theatre and Barbican, 2008); *Chatroom* (Cottesloe, Royal National Theatre, March, 2006 and Autumn, 2007); *The Small Things* (for Paines Plough, Menier Chocolate Factory, London and Galway Arts Festival, 2005); *The New Electric Ballroom* (Kammerspiele Theater Munich, winner of Theater Heute's Best Foreign Play, 2005); two short plays, *How These Men Talk* (Zurich Shauspielehaus) and *Lynndie's Gotta Gun* (for Artistas Unidos, Lisbon's National Theatre); *bedbound* (Dublin Theatre Festival, 2000; Edinburgh, 2001 – Fringe First Winner; Royal Court, London; New York and worldwide); *Misterman* (for Corcadorca, Granary Theatre, Cork, 1999); *Disco Pigs* (for Corcadorca, Triskel, Cork, 1995; Dublin, 1996; Edinburgh, 1997; West End, 1998 – awarded Arts Council Playwrights Award, 1996, Best Fringe Production, 1996, Stewart Parker and George Devine Awards, 1997); *The Ginger Ale Boy* (for Corcadorca, Cork, 1994).

Film: *Chatroom* (Ruby Films/FILMFOUR); *Hunger* (Blast/FILMFOUR, winner of the Camera D'Or and international prize in Cannes, 2008); *Disco Pigs* (Temple Films/ Renaissance).

In Development: *Island of the Aunts* (an adaptation of Eva Ibbotson's children's novel for Cuba Pictures); *Dusty Springfield: Goddess of the Sixties* (Number 9 Films/FILMFOUR); *Into that Darkness* (Element/ FILMFOUR).

Radio: *Four Big Days in the Life of Dessie Banks* (RTÉ Radio – winner of the PPI Award for Best Radio Drama, 2001); *The Monotonous Life of Little Miss P* (BBC – commended in the Berlin Prix Europa, 2003).

Awards: Enda Walsh's plays have been performed worldwide and have been translated into more than twenty languages. He has received an Obie Award (2010) for *The New Electric Ballroom*, the Edinburgh Herald Archangel Award (2008) for his contribution to the Edinburgh Festival Fringe, four Edinburgh Fringe First Awards as well as a Critic's Choice Award (1997).

MIKEL MURFI Director

Mikel trained at École Jacques Lecoq, Paris and is from Sligo.

Druid: As an actor, *The New Electric Ballroom*, *Lynndie's Gotta Gun*, *The Increased Difficulty of Concentration*. As a director, *The Walworth Farce*.

Other theatre: As an actor, *The Chairs* (Blue Raincoat, Sligo); *The Cure* (Half Moon Theatre, Cork); *The Clerk and the Clown* (Galway Arts Festival); *Playing A Round* (Galway Arts Festival); *The Morning After Optimism*, *The Playboy of the Western World* (Peacock Theatre); *The Tempest*, *The Comedy of Errors* (Abbey Theatre); *Stokehauling*, *SickDyingDeadBuriedOut*, *Half Eight Mass of a Tuesday*, *Come Down from the Mountain John Clown John Clown*, *Macbeth*, *God's Gift*, *The White Headed Boy* (Barabbas); *Studs*, *Melting Penguins* (Passion Machine); *Lady Windermere's Fan* (Rough Magic); *The Tender Trap* (Pigsback). As a director: *Diamonds in the Soil*, *The Lost Days of Ollie Deasy* (Macnas); *The Mysteries* (Co-director, Macnas); *Trad* (Galway Arts Festival Production); *The Lonesome West* (Lyric Theatre, Belfast); *Falling Out of Love* (Yew Tree Theatre).

Film & Television: As an actor, *Ella Enchanted*, *The Last September*, *Sweety Barrett*, *The Butcher Boy*, *Love and Rage*, *Guiltrip*, *Words Upon The Window Pane*, *The Three Joes*, *The Commitments*, *The Ballad of Kid Kanturk*. As a director: *Druma* (a short film for Macnas); *John Duffy's Brother* (for Parkfilms based on the Flann O'Brien short story, screenplay by Eoghan Nolan).

SABINE DARGENT Designer

Sabine is a French designer living in Ireland.

Druid: *The New Electric Ballroom*, *The Walworth Farce* (Irish Times Theatre Award for Best Set Design, 2006).

Other theatre: *Strandline*, *The Pride of Parnell Street* (Dublin, London, New Haven); *Monged*, *Pilgrims in the Park*, *Tadhg Stray Wandered In* (Fishamble); *Circus* (Dublin, New Haven – Barabbas); *City Fusion* (St Patrick's Parade 2008, 9 and 10); *The Lonesome West* (Ireland); *The Bacchae of Baghdad*, *The Importance of Being Earnest* (Abbey Theatre); *Antigone*, *Hard to Believe* (Storytellers Theatre Co); *Henry and Harriet* (Belfast); *To Have and to Hold* (Old Museum, Belfast); *Days of Wine and Roses* (Ireland); *Dublin Carol* (Ireland); *Ghosts* (ESB/Irish Times Best Set Design Award, 2003); *How Many Miles to Babylon?*, *The Merchant of Venice*, *A Doll's House* (Second Age); *The Shadow of the Glen*, *The Tinker's Wedding* (Big Telly); *Martha*, *Little Rudolf* (Barnstorm); *Jack Fell Down*, *Burning Dreams*, *Last Call* (Team); *The Tempest* (Blue Raincoat); *Desert Lullaby* (Gallowglass); *Hysteria* (B*spoke). Sabine has also worked with Theatre A Grande Vitesse (Paris), Théâtre de Châtillon and L'Epée de Bois in France.

PAUL KEOGAN Lighting Designer

Born in Ireland, Paul studied Drama at Trinity College Dublin and at Glasgow University.

Druid: *The Walworth Farce, The Spirit of Annie Ross.*

Other theatre: *Wake* (Nationale Reisopera, Netherlands); *No Escape, The Resistible Rise of Arturo Ui, Romeo and Juliet, Ages of the Moon* (Dublin, Atlantic Theatre NYC); *Julius Caesar* (Abbey Theatre); *Plasticine, MedEia, The Hairy Ape, Woyzeck* (Corcadorca); *Les Liaisons Dangereuses, The Deep Blue Sea, The Birds* (Gate Theatre, Dublin); *Intemperance* (Everyman, Liverpool); *Tartuffe* (Liverpool Playhouse); *The Taming of the Shrew* (Royal Shakespeare Company); *Harvest* (Royal Court Theatre); *born bad* (Hampstead Theatre); *Blue/Orange* (Crucible Theatre, Sheffield); *Pierrot Lunaire* (Almeida Opera); *Angel/Babel* (Operating Theatre); *Trad* (Galway Arts Festival); *The Makropulos Case, Der Fliegende Holländer* (Opera Zuid, Netherlands); *Transformations* (Wexford Festival Opera); *Die Zauberflöte* (National Opera of Korea); *Lady Macbeth of Mtensk* (Opera Ireland).

GREGORY CLARKE Sound Designer

Druid: *The New Electric Ballroom, The Hackney Office.*

Other theatre: *Hedda Gabler* (Theatre Royal, Bath); *A Midsummer Night's Dream, Treasure Island* (Rose Theatre, Kingston); *Bay* (Young Vic); *Loot* (Tricycle, Theatre Royal, Newcastle); *The Vortex* (Apollo Theatre); *Ring Round the Moon* (Playhouse Theatre); *Cloud Nine* (Almeida Theatre); *Pygmalion* (American Airlines, Broadway); *Equus, And Then There Were None, Some Girls* (Gielgud Theatre); *Journey's End* (London, UK tour and Broadway – New York Drama Desk Award winner for Outstanding Sound Design); *A Voyage Round My Father, Honour* (Wyndham's Theatre); *The Philanthropist* (Donmar Warehouse); *Hayfever, Lady Windermere's Fan, The Royal Family* (Theatre Royal, Haymarket); *The Home Place, Whose Life is it Anyway?* (Comedy Theatre); *The Emperor Jones, The Chairs* (Gate Theatre, London); *Waiting for Godot, Abigail's Party* (New Ambassadors Theatre); *What the Butler Saw* (Criterion Theatre); *Six Degrees of Separation, The Dresser* (Duke of York's Theatre); *Amy's View, You Never Can Tell* (Garrick Theatre); *National Anthems* (Old Vic); *Betrayal* (Duchess Theatre); *Mum's the Word* (Albery Theatre); *Song of Singapore* (Mayfair Theatre); *No Man's Land, Tristan and Yseult, The Emperor Jones* (National Theatre); *Great Expectations, Coriolanus, The Merry Wives of Windsor, Tantalus and Cymbeline* (RSC); *Troilus and Cressida* (European tour); *The English Game* (UK tour); *Blackbird* (UK tour); *Crown Matrimonial* (UK tour); *Uncle Vanya* (Rose, Kingston); *Pygmalion, Little Nell, Measure for Measure, Habeas Corpus, Miss Julie, Private Lives, Much Ado About Nothing, You Can Never Tell, Design for Living, Betrayal, Fight for Barbara, As You Like It* (Peter Hall Company); *The Changeling* (Barbican); *Nights at the Circus* (Lyric Theatre, Hammersmith, and tour); *Insignificance* (Sheffield Lyceum); *My Boy Jack* (UK tour).

Awards: 2009 Tony Award for Best Sound Design for *Equus.*

PENELOPE

Enda Walsh

Characters

BURNS, *mid-thirties*
QUINN, *mid-forties*
DUNNE, *about fifty*
FITZ, *mid-sixties*

...*and* PENELOPE, *twenties*

This text went to press before the end of rehearsals and so may differ slightly from the play as performed.

After a little time we realise that we're looking at a dilapidated swimming pool drained of water. There are two ladders at the back of the pool where the actors enter.

At the back and above the swimming pool we can see a large sliding glass door that leads into a villa. There's a scrim which allows us to see inside, when appropriate.

The pool's been turned into a living space and it seems to have operated as such for years.

There are five battered pool loungers of different makes and sizes (some inflatable), a miniature snooker table, a trestle table stacked with beer, wine, spirits and snacks. There's a portable CD stereo. There's also a large helium-filled heart-shaped balloon bobbing above the table. Under the table there's a mass of junk.

There's a standing screen, at the back in the corner, large enough for someone to change behind it unseen.

There's a large gleaming Taunton Deluxe Barbecue raised on a wooden pallet in the very centre of the pool.

Most importantly there's a CCTV camera in the pool looking down at the men.

When the lights come up we have time to take all this in as the two men on stage are very still. We could be looking at a picture.

One of the men is standing beside one of the ladders holding a sponge full of pink suds. He's been cleaning a long streak of blood off the tiled wall by the ladder and stands there staring at the drips coming down the wall.

This is BURNS.

A man in his mid-thirties, he wears a short Terrycloth swimming-pool robe, scruffy trainers and battered spectacles. He looks strong and able but carries himself subserviently.

The other man is standing looking intensely at the Taunton Deluxe Barbecue.

This is QUINN.

He's a powerfully built, mid-forties man. His dyed black hair perfectly set, he's immediately a man of some vanity. He's wearing tight red Speedos and a pair of smart brown moccasins.

The stillness is broken when QUINN *quickly walks to the barbecue.* BURNS *turns to look at him.*

QUINN *reaches out his hand and holds it above the grill to test its temperature. As usual it's cold. There's an uncooked sausage on the grill. He picks it up and looks at it. He drops it back down.*

He walks quickly back to the trestle table, stops and throws a look at BURNS.

BURNS *hesitates. He was about to say something but decides not to.* QUINN *wants to hear it.*

QUINN. What do you have to say? (*Slight pause.*) What is it?

A pause. BURNS *gathers the courage.*

BURNS. I need to talk about Murray.

QUINN *puts on the stereo and Herb Alpert and the Tijuana Brass play 'Spanish Flea'.*

QUINN *finds a blowtorch amongst the snacks. He turns back and looks at the defunct barbecue like he means business. The blowtorch fires in his hand. He walks back over to the barbecue and begins blasting the sausage. He's cooking it for breakfast.*

BURNS *drops the sponge into his metal bucket. He can't get rid of the last of the blood on the wall. He returns the bucket to under the trestle table. He starts to look for something on top of the table. He finds it and puts it on. It's a cardboard cone-shaped party hat that elasticates under his chin.*

At the same time two other men appear and climb down the two ladders at the back. They're also dressed in Terrycloth swimming-pool robes.

As they turn to us we see DUNNE.

A man of about fifty. He carries himself like an old theatrical troubadour (in flip-flops). He goes straight to the table to fix himself a cocktail, ignoring BURNS *completely. He dances a little to the music for his own entertainment. He can move.*

The other man is FITZ.

A trim and fidgety mid-sixties man. He carefully organises his pool lounger and towel. Everything has to be in its place. He's brought an old book to read and takes real care that his bookmark is doing its job. He has a small container of tablets. He empties the contents out. There's only three tablets in there. That will do. He throws them into his mouth and knocks back a bottle of tomato juice. He blesses himself. That was the wrong direction. He tries it again and again but has forgotten how to bless himself. He gives up. His manner's a little fey.

DUNNE *meanwhile has fixed his cocktail. It's a very flamboyant margarita topped with fruit and tiny paper umbrellas. He walks over to watch* QUINN *pulverising the sausage.*

BURNS *remains at the table where he's placed various snacks into various bowls. He acts as a reluctant servant throughout.*

FITZ *acknowledges him with a little nod.* FITZ *turns and looks at the blood on the wall.* BURNS *does the same.*

The two men then look over at QUINN.

QUINN *turns off the blowtorch and hands it to* DUNNE.

He reaches into the barbecue and grabs the sausage but burns his hand.

QUINN. Shit!

BURNS *doesn't have to be asked. He comes to the barbecue, grabs the ferociously hot sausage and starts to blow on it for* QUINN.

A perfect temperature now and QUINN *finally takes the sausage in his hand as 'Spanish Flea' comes to an end.*

*The men speak with considerable erudition. They may be of different classes (*QUINN *is certainly a rougher diamond) but they all like the sound of their own voice. Their accents are provincial (each one from a different area of the country) though sound soft... as these are men of distinction.*

5

QUINN *bites into the sausage.*

DUNNE. How is it?

A pause as QUINN *carefully chooses his word.*

QUINN. 'Sausagey.'

DUNNE. That's good.

FITZ (*to* DUNNE). Most are often not. Some are. Some have got a sausageness but more often than not they taste of nothing but heat.

DUNNE. And heat isn't even a taste.

FITZ. Isn't it?

DUNNE. People would say that heat was a sensation, you know… generally…

QUINN. As a rule.

DUNNE. As you say, Quinn… as a rule… the word having its meanings… having its related characteristics, Fitz. 'What does heat have?' 'Taste' is not the first thing that springs to mind.

QUINN. 'This tastes hot.' I would say that before I would say this tastes of sausage.

DUNNE. But I said, 'How is it?' and you said, 'Sausagey.' Why didn't you say that it tastes hot if hot was your first sensation?

QUINN. Hot was my first sensation but I said 'sausagey' out of badness.

DUNNE. Right.

QUINN. This is the very last sausage, men, and I wanted you all to know that it's a superior sausage. Not some dust-filled, cigar-shaped, hunk of pigshit… but an actual sausage! The sausage of our youth. Had I just said, 'This is a hot sausage'… well, that has negative connotations…

FITZ. Not if we were cold, it doesn't. A hot sausage would be quite nice in the cold!

QUINN. Obviously not if we were cold, Fitz. Had we been sitting in a yurt in Mongolia shivering into a herd of yaks and

I was clutching this sausage… I would look you each in the eye and smile… 'Gentlemen, this is a hot sausage! The last hot sausage! The final sausage, heated! What do you feel about that then, lads?'

FITZ. Jealous. And cold.

DUNNE. Leaning in trying to get a modicum of heat off that delicious-looking banger, no doubt.

QUINN. But this is not Mongolia…

FITZ *and* DUNNE. God, no…!

QUINN. …this is… Burns!

BURNS. What?

QUINN. What is this?

BURNS. A sausage?

QUINN. Yes, it's a sausage! What are we here?

BURNS. 11.30 a.m.

QUINN. More importantly!

BURNS. Thirty-three degrees Celsius.

FITZ. That's hot.

DUNNE. That's hot and early.

BURNS. It's always hot.

DUNNE. And invariably early…! (*Trails off.*) …when it isn't late…

QUINN. And this… my fellow competitors… this is sausagey.

QUINN *starts to eat the sausage as the others look at him.*

The early bird, men… early bird…

QUINN *begins to nibble at the sausage, impersonating an early bird until it disappears into his mouth. He swallows.*

Done.

QUINN *opens his mouth to show that it is gone.* DUNNE *inspects it.*

DUNNE. Even after all this time, the competition.

QUINN. What else is there?

DUNNE. You're right.

QUINN. There's nothing else!

DUNNE. I need to be reminded of that on a daily basis so as to maintain my edge!

QUINN. You do.

DUNNE. I didn't have to do that as a younger man, we all remember that! My body still holds a physical memory of the attack of my youth but the mind wavers. It's a waverer!

FITZ. The mind is the enemy!

DUNNE. The mind is a bucket of eels, lads! It obviously is with us four, given our emmm... What would you call it?

QUINN. Situation.

DUNNE. Given our remarkable situation. I am an afternoon away from turning to jelly... so it's important to remember that the fight is still on, lads!

QUINN. It most certainly is.

DUNNE. Good!

> QUINN *glances over at* BURNS *who stares at the blood on the back wall.* DUNNE *shows a coin to* QUINN. *He waves his other hand over it and it disappears.*

QUINN. Seen it.

FITZ. Must say there's some days I'd welcome the degeneration. A life in jelly doesn't sound that bad. I'd miss reading of course. Conversation you can keep. Words are cheap, Dunne...

DUNNE. Cheap and nasty.

FITZ....but reading... the classics in particular... the companionship of Homer...

DUNNE. I never read a book in my adult life.

FITZ. That surprises me!

8

QUINN. Nor me.

FITZ. Well, that's less surprising really…

QUINN *didn't like that insult.*

DUNNE. There was only ever one book I cared for as a boy.

FITZ. And what was that?

DUNNE. *The Magic Porridge Pot.*

QUINN. That's the only book there is.

FITZ. There are others actually.

QUINN. Not that speak so clearly of investment and growth or the fast development of an unstable economy.

DUNNE. Oh, right?

QUINN. This is a whole town that ground to a standstill when it became awash with porridge, yeah…

DUNNE. Interesting.

QUINN. …a pot that gave and gave, a community that took with no notion of responsibility or future.

FITZ. I thought the magic porridge pot lifted the people out of poverty.

DUNNE. And into obesity, those fat bastards!

QUINN. Can you imagine eating yourself through porridge 'cause you can't get out of first gear? Or imagine the consistency of a heart fed on a diet of sweet stodgy oats. Jaysus!

FITZ. Crikey.

QUINN. What the pot needed was regulation. It needed that little girl to stay at home with the sole purpose of saying, 'Cook-pot-cook' and 'Stop-pot-stop'. Outside of that she didn't need any more words.

FITZ. She would have grown up retarded, mind you.

QUINN. She would have grown up in power.

DUNNE. She'd be the keeper of the pot.

QUINN. Exactly! She'd be the keeper of the pot.

DUNNE. Fascinating read!

QUINN. Lovely pictures!

FITZ. Which is the reason why I'd miss reading! It's that type of mental stimulation, that access to ideas and colour and character! Without this book, without this unequivocal bond between me and it… (*He kisses his book.*) I imagine a hellish jelly! Absolutely hellish! And yet for all of that there's still a lot of pluses to senility as it's such a huge effort to maintain the fight, isn't that right, boys?

DUNNE. You forget the prize.

FITZ. You do forget the prize. You, Burns? Do you forget?

BURNS. Do I forget what?

QUINN. The prize!

BURNS. No.

DUNNE. I can't either.

QUINN. Nor me.

FITZ. Or me! I wish I could. I lie to myself that I can but of course I can't. I'll tease myself with the notion of senility, distract myself with Homer but really, truthfully… of course I can't forget the prize.

DUNNE grabs a hold of his stomach and moves it slowly. The others watch.

He stops and picks his drink back up.

DUNNE. It's impossible to say exactly what physical shape I would have morphed into had my journey sent me elsewhere. What a fascinating thing the body is, gents.

FITZ. Remarkable, really.

DUNNE. And your body, Fitz? Tell me and tell me with honesty now… do you lament the obvious muscle wastage, your kindling-like bone structure, the fact that your skin resembles a shrunken piece of yellowing parchment?

FITZ. Somewhere on life's journey the body goes its separate way. My head reconciled a few years ago that I was no longer 'the man that I was', Dunne.

DUNNE. Very wise.

FITZ. Something your head must have done in its youth, what with your...?

DUNNE. With my...?

FITZ. With your considerable...

DUNNE. My considerable what...?!

FITZ. Your considerable geography...

DUNNE. [*'I understand you.'*] I have you.

QUINN. The day the head and body part company is a tragic day for the self. I am what I was in my early twenties, exactly the same, lads... like some sensuous ninja. Beyond that! Improved upon! Controlled. You treat the body with respect and in return it will repay the head a thousand per cent.

DUNNE. Percentages aside, Quinn, I will always allow my body to take the lead over the wavering head. This is the man I am!

QUINN. All stomach, you mean.

DUNNE. It's the gut that's led my life, that powers my performances here in this pool.

QUINN. Gotcha.

DUNNE. Of course I'd be a more svelte animal had I had a more emm... a more ahh...?

FITZ. A more productive existence?

DUNNE. As you say... but the body must be respected for what the body wishes and the head must support the body, not unlike the lowly oxpecker bird who must feed on the back of the obscenely large hippopotamus. The body, boys... the body is always the king.

QUINN. Or kingdom.

DUNNE. Or kingdom, yes, Quinn. Depending on one's...

BURNS. Appetite. Depending on one's appetite the body is one's king or kingdom.

DUNNE *fires* BURNS *a look. He's spoken out of turn. Slight pause.*

DUNNE. A dictum you may put to use one day, my boy. Looking a little peaky this morning.

BURNS. 'Peaky'?

DUNNE. Like a bulimic buck after a long day's frolicking.

BURNS. Okay.

DUNNE. Like an emaciated kidney after a long day's filtering.

BURNS. Understood.

DUNNE. Get a sandwich into you. Where's the Twiglets?

BURNS. The table.

DUNNE. Fetch 'em then!

BURNS *hesitates. Not to go would make things worse.*

DUNNE, *for some reason, does a fantastical flamenco step.*

BURNS *goes and fetches the bowl of Twiglets for* DUNNE. *He returns with the bowl and hands it to* DUNNE.

Divert your eyes, ya scamp!

BURNS *doesn't. It's quite a moment.* FITZ *and* QUINN *turn and look.*

BURNS *and* DUNNE *stare into each other's eyes. If anything,* BURNS *is being the more aggressive.* DUNNE *picks up a Twiglet and quickly turns away from* BURNS *with the bowl.*

FITZ *returns to Homer and is immediately engrossed in the book.*

FITZ (*whispers to himself about a certain piece of text*). Very very good.

QUINN *walks to the back wall and looks at the bloodstain on the tiles. He begins to do some press-ups against the wall, his face centimetres from the blood.*

BURNS *watches him until he can't any longer.*

Out of frustration, BURNS *suddenly slaps his own face. SCHLAP! They all look at him.*

BURNS. What?

FITZ (*noticing* BURNS*'s party hat*). Is it the weekend already?

DUNNE. Well, the hat's on, so it must be.

FITZ. Where does time go, hey, Burns!?

BURNS. Turns into cancer apparently.

DUNNE. Only seems like yesterday that it was yesterday.

BURNS. It was yesterday.

DUNNE. I was right then. Right again!

BURNS. Right.

QUINN. Time's a tragedy, men.

FITZ. Hey, my mammy used to say that! That exact phrase, 'Time's a tragedy.'

QUINN (*sarcastic*). Well, fancy that! So did my mother!

FITZ. We might have had the same mother, Quinn!

QUINN. We could have done, I suppose.

FITZ. Of course we would have met in childhood, right?

QUINN. Not necessarily, I never mixed with my family.

FITZ. Oh, that's an interesting psychological fact!

QUINN. It was a joke.

FITZ (*laughing*). Oh, very good! Very clever.

DUNNE (*laughing*). A very funny joke, Quinn. Very funny humour!

QUINN (*cold*). Right.

FITZ. Well, she was never a woman for words, my mother. She could talk but I was always of the opinion that she hated the debris that conversation left behind. She couldn't see the point of offering an opinion on anything!

13

QUINN. Your mother was a woman, right?

FITZ. Oh, completely! And rather than thinking of her as a halfwit, I like to think of her as a revolutionary! Had her ideas on vocal abstinence caught on, you could imagine, boys, a world with absolutely no wars. Or had there been wars they would be enacted through mime...

QUINN mixes a cocktail like a professional.

...a quiet, sparse, thoughtful world devoid of the yap yap but unfortunately populated with the leotard and the whitened face of the mime artiste.

DUNNE. A wonderful illusion, mime!

DUNNE begins performing some mime as the others look on. He plays a man trapped in a box.

QUINN. Every empire has its price to pay, Mr Fitz.

FITZ. Yes, that's very true.

QUINN opens an invisible door on the invisible box.

QUINN. Get out.

DUNNE steps out.

FITZ. Was your mother brilliant in any way, Dunne?

DUNNE. 'Brilliant', no. God, no! She left little imprint on the world, my mother, except for her size. She was a fat lady and unpleasant with it. I was still wetting my bed as a teenager and I put that down to a total absence of physical affection. I found the only way to get a hug off her was to season my neck with a little gravy.

FITZ. Mothers and sons, will we ever escape their influence!

DUNNE (*grandly*). Books will be written! Plays will be expelled... and the great mystery of mother and son will continue to baffle like the mystery of yeast!

QUINN. What are we going to do about this fucking barbecue?

FITZ and DUNNE walk over to QUINN, and the three men look at the barbecue like it was a spaceship.

Finally...

BURNS. You could kill it.

QUINN *turns and looks at* BURNS.

QUINN. It still holds promise. Still has hope for us.

DUNNE. What does man have but 'hope', Burns.

BURNS. Fuel would help.

FITZ. It did fire that very first time... when was that?

QUINN. A few years back.

FITZ. As long ago as that!?

DUNNE. Remember how it came, all wrapped up and addressed to us, in our names?

FITZ. Oh yes, that was a great day!

QUINN. It was, yeah.

FITZ. I miss that day.

DUNNE. The box was in the middle just here... or perhaps there... and we had no idea how it got down, remember. A crane. God's hand. A team of magical fairies dedicated to outdoor cooking. It was mysterious and extraordinary, wasn't it, lads?! And so we awoke from our *fata Morgana* and stood perusing the box and discussing in detail its removal. In time we agreed on a procedure and then we carefully lifted the box upwards to reveal this stunning barbecue... not unlike the historic moment Howard Carter unsealed the doorway into Tutankhamun's burial chamber. Wonderful. (*Slight pause.*) And then we put Burns in the box for a little bit.

BURNS. For a day.

DUNNE. A day!?

QUINN (*smiling*). It was a day and a night.

BURNS. You taped the box back up and left me in there for twenty-four hours.

FITZ. That was a little cruel. Are you sure?

BURNS. Yes, I'm sure.

FITZ. And why did we do that, I wonder?

15

DUNNE *and* QUINN *are laughing.*

BURNS. Boredom probably, I don't know, I couldn't hear the conversation. I was concealed in a mountain of foam peanuts like a plastic toy in a Kellogg's box.

DUNNE (*losing it*). Holy God!

QUINN. We were excited though, right?!

DUNNE. Beyond excitement!

QUINN. We let you out in the morning and apologised.

DUNNE. And you accepted our apology.

BURNS. That's right, I did.

FITZ. Well, that's good! (*Praising* BURNS.) And gracious.

DUNNE. But it was a mystery, wasn't it?

FITZ. It was.

DUNNE. The sender unknown, and me and Fitz and Murray sat about speculating the sender's identity while Quinn fired up the barbecue. Oh, we had big dreams then! Massive! I'd imagined us standing around like a group of friends, eating hot meats, drinking cool beers, talking business into the early hours.

QUINN. But it farted out a tiny fire and has since been extinguished. Bastard.

DUNNE. It's a garden tragedy, is what it is! A real bastard!

FITZ. We should have removed it a long time ago. It's actually mocking us by sitting here! It's placing unworkable images in our heads, boys. It's a pornography!

DUNNE. I hate that fucking barbecue!

FITZ. Might we get rid of it, Quinn? Please!

QUINN. We'd never get it up the ladder.

DUNNE. Have we ever tried?

BURNS. You made me try once.

DUNNE. And what was the outcome?

BURNS. A slipped disc.

QUINN. I had a dream about it last night. Dreamt that it was on
fire.

A long pause. The other three are immediately in shock.
QUINN *turns and sees this.*

(*Carefully.*) What is it?

DUNNE. I dreamt that too.

QUINN *on edge now.*

FITZ. And me too, Quinn.

The stage is charged with fear. QUINN, FITZ *and* DUNNE
look at BURNS.

QUINN. And you?

BURNS. What?!

QUINN. You had a dream last night. Did you see the barbecue
on fire?

FITZ. You know what it means if you have...?!

DUNNE. Just say it if you have!

QUINN. Did you have the dream or not, Burns!

BURNS. Yes! (*Slight pause.*) At the start of my dream it was on
fire.

A pause. They are all shook, terrified.

FITZ. So tell the dream.

A pause.

QUINN. The fire starts underneath the barbecue. It starts at the
same time he steps from his boat onto the shore and looks up
at the house here. The fire fills the barbecue's frame as his feet
take to the sharp rocks. He glances over at our white houses
huddled together by the cove, creaking and empty. He could
crumble them with a breath but he couldn't be bothered, he
wants us and our blood. He knows what we've turned his
house into, how we spend our days here in his pool. How
Penelope sits in that room watching us... doubting that he's

17

alive maybe… and maybe choosing one of us for love. This is our hope, our religion… but today her husband returns. (*Slight pause*.) The barbecue he must have sent it to taunt us… it burns and he's here. (*Slight pause*.) He's running up the pathway, the cypress and hyacinth heavy in the middle of the day, they fill his head and wipe out in an instant his years of exile, of war, of the journey home to her… the longing for Penelope. He's over the parched grass now and smelling the poisonous barbecue snaking up into the air and he can hear us in the pool. She's standing there with happy tears in her eyes but he doesn't go to her but to us and to his knife. And if only it were quick but he's in amongst us ripping apart our legs and we're scurrying about the floor like whingeing bloodied slugs. He pulls Fitz aside and makes us watch. He fillets him. And how easy the blade cuts him up. He shatters his old bones with his hands. He moves… hacking up limbs and tossing innards aside like he's looking for something in Fitz. Flesh is landing on the grill, the barbecue mocking us this final time. And Fitz is falling in and out of consciousness but he's slapping him awake, he's spitting beer in his face, he wants to see his eyes, have Fitz see what he sees. He cracks open Fitz's chest, reaches in and takes his heart in his hand. (*Slight pause*.) And their eyes lock together now… and he squeezes his heart slowly. Ever so slowly. (*Pause*.) He's looking at one of us three. He's smiling. And we're next.

A pause.

Is that how we all saw it?

FITZ *and* DUNNE *nod*.

QUINN *looks at* BURNS.

BURNS. Yes.

QUINN. Right. Then it will be today.

DUNNE (*barely audible*). My God.

A pause.

FITZ. I never thought I'd have the backbone for suicide but faced now with the likelihood of watching my own backbone being removed and flung onto that barbecue, I think it's only fair that I should give suicide a shot.

DUNNE. A shot we can't do... we have knives though.

FITZ (*panicking*). Why didn't these knives feature in our dream as weapons of defence?!

DUNNE. Courage, Fitz, courage!

FITZ. I'm pretty handy with a knife! I whittled a penny whistle out of some beechwood once. Beechwood as we all know is a very hard wood and the blasted thing took me the best part of my summer holidays to carve. When I went to play it... it whistled like a dying breath. Exactly the same noise... and a similar stench. But knives I can do, Quinn!

BURNS. I don't want to die in that pain! Not by him, not here, not today!

QUINN. And you won't die!

BURNS. There's nothing we can do, Quinn!

DUNNE. We arm ourselves, is what we do!

QUINN. We do not arm ourselves! We know the man we're dealing with here! This man is a colossus! This is a man who went to war and butchered thousands without breaking sweat.

BURNS (*retching*). Oh God...

QUINN. A bowel movement sends us into palpitations! This is a legend who faced monsters, who remained unblinking, unfazed before he humiliated them into submission. Dunne has a phobia for autumn.

DUNNE. You say 'a phobia', I call it 'a legitimate fear'!

QUINN. It's a season!

DUNNE. It's a decaying, withering slow walk into the darkness of winter, is what it is!

QUINN. Stop it now!

DUNNE. Death I can do but the journey towards death, the long walk... The thievery of autumn when we are robbed of summer sunshine and led further into the depression of a dying year...

BURNS. Fuck it, I need a drink!

QUINN (*to* BURNS). Behave yourself now! Don't you dare drink!

BURNS *goes to table and hits the spirits fast.*

FITZ (*to* DUNNE). I never thought of autumn like that! You spoke there with the clarity of a great poet. I always had you pigeon-holed as a Master Derivative but now I see that actually I have neither a pigeon or a hole. For the rest of our days you are indescribable to me, Dunne.

DUNNE. Thank you.

FITZ. Of course there's a certainty that we're talking minutes rather than days…

DUNNE. Quite.

FITZ. And yet in those minutes you will be a laureate of our times!

DUNNE. My mother would be proud… had she not been a fat heartless bitch.

FITZ. Fix me a very large G and T, Dunne!

DUNNE. It would be my pleasure. (*Calls.*) Burns, fix him a sup!

BURNS. If we leave, we leave to nowhere! This island is miniscule! We hide in our houses and he'd sniff us out. We could row but we've already sold our boats for beer.

DUNNE (*outraged*). And not gin?!

BURNS. We could fashion together a vessel using our recliners… only to perish on the reef. None of us can swim!

FITZ. The irony being is that we've spent the worst part of our lives in a swimming pool!

BURNS. We are fucked and no amount of comedy is going to lessen that fact, Fitz!

FITZ. I am using levity, young man, as a tonic to see us through the next few moments before Quinn delivers to us a plan of action!

They're all hitting the alcohol to calm down.

DUNNE. Remember it was Fitz that he will fillet first. It will be Fitz that he will prepare for the barbecue!

FITZ. That's right!

DUNNE. And yet is Fitz wading through the doldrums of his subconscious?! Is it Fitz who is wandering aimlessly through the forest of disenchantment… sailing a sea of desolation… No, it is not Burns because Fitz is an Optimist…!

BURNS. A Cockeyed Optimist.

FITZ. I may very well be a little cockeyed…

DUNNE. In a certain light…

FITZ. In a certain light certainly… But I am happy!

DUNNE. You're also a little high.

BURNS. You're medicated.

FITZ. Yes. Extremely medicated.

BURNS. Do you have any more?

FITZ. Sadly only three pills entered my decaying belly. 'The Father, the Son and the Holy Ghost.'

BURNS. FUCK!

FITZ. Indeed. Quinn?

QUINN. We stay.

QUINN *turns to them.*

We do as we always do. Everything will change if Penelope agrees to take one of us as her husband today. If she does… he's left bobbing about the ocean like flotsam. The dream will have come to us and not to her. So it is a day like any other day. We sell our love to her as we do always but today with the support of the others. It is in our interest that someone at least wins her… so we work together, men.

BURNS. 'Together'? Us?! Oh, what shit…! SHIT SHIT!

QUINN (*to* BURNS). Enough!

BURNS *gulps down the spirits and shovels in the snacks.*

FITZ. You're joking! The sort of men we are, Quinn! This is a joke, right?!

QUINN (*grabbing* FITZ*'s head like a hypnotist*). Gather all that you are, Fitz. Gather it, gather it!

FITZ. Right.

QUINN. Take every instinct, every impulse, everything you believe yourself to be and stand for. Take it, digest it!

FITZ. Done.

QUINN. Now shit it out! From this moment on we build anew, lads!

FITZ. A new what? What are we building?!

DUNNE. A company!

FITZ. An actual company!?

DUNNE. It is a company, right?

QUINN. Exactly…

DUNNE. A group of men with a common ideology, a collective direction! That's what you're suggesting, Quinn! We're building a company right here!

FITZ. Do we get to wear a uniform?

QUINN. We don't have time for that.

DUNNE. A motto! A motto's essential! Possibly in Latin.

BURNS. '*Is Res Non Vos Es Caro In A Assus*.'

FITZ. Meaning?

BURNS. 'It Matters Not, We Are Meat On A Barbecue.'

QUINN *slaps* BURNS *across the head with a table-tennis bat*.

FITZ. But how can I be certain that we are together? Could I really trust Dunne, for example?

DUNNE. The old Dunne – no.

FITZ. No.

DUNNE. No one could trust the old Dunne. I myself have had issues of trust with my very self – the old Dunne who has buried his morality beneath this festering pool. But the new Dunne that stands before you like a veritable Apostle of Goodness...

BURNS. In flip-flops.

DUNNE. In flip-flops, correct... I am at one with you, Mr Fitz. You can go beyond trusting me. You can erase the meaning of 'trust' in your heavily fingered dictionary and supplant it with my very own face.

FITZ (*backing away*). Jeepers.

QUINN. Embrace it, Fitz!

FITZ (*it's new to his mouth*). Embrace 'trust'??

DUNNE (*holding out his arms*). Embrace 'trust'!

QUINN *and* FITZ *talk to each other as* DUNNE *slowly approaches, arms outstretched.*

QUINN. Though every fibre of your being – (*Pointing at* DUNNE.) recoils at even the sight of this man...

FITZ. Yes...

QUINN. Although you probably heave as I too heave at Dunne's efforts of seduction... Today in front of Penelope we stand beside Dunne!

DUNNE. Embrace me, Fitz!

QUINN. His success is our life...

FITZ. Oh God...

DUNNE. Support, respect and unite around me, men!

FITZ. It won't be easy.

QUINN. It will be very difficult.

FITZ. Especially with Dunne.

QUINN. It will be agony.

DUNNE. But how men build and how we survive! Sure, aren't we wired for change. If not we'd still be communing with those hairy apes.

BURNS. Some of us have no choice!

QUINN. Some of us are more comfortable in the company of monkeys… subservient-bespectacled-little shitheads! But not us three! Not now!

FITZ *embraces* DUNNE.

FITZ. We are company!

QUINN (*chuffed*). We are company, Mr Fitz!

BURNS*'s head drops.*

DUNNE. We are one voice! Now gather! GATHER!

QUINN *points up to the CCTV camera. It's pivoting and looking down at them.*

QUINN. You're playing for our lives, Dunne! Seduce well… and may the gods spare us!

The red light goes on on the camera and a follow spot beams down on DUNNE.

The beautiful PENELOPE *can immediately be seen through the scrim, sitting in a seat and watching a large television and the live transmission inside the villa.*

DUNNE*'s on. He steps up to a microphone and looks to the camera.*

In seduction, DUNNE *is even more outlandishly theatrical.*

DUNNE. You wake! And down the hill across the cove, through my little blue door, into my Crackerbread house… I too awake, Penel… ope. Somehow your first morning's breath rides the treacherous wind and finds its way to my own nose and awakens me! (*He smells.*) And it is a fine breath! Not the claggy-acid-breath of a stomach made stagnant by a night's sleep… the type of breath that could peel a hard-boiled egg… oh fuck, no! But a breath that perfumers would battle to bottle. A breath bursting with pheromones! Is it any wonder it builds a mighty tower in my underpants. A tower that I take to the shower and lather with peasant olive soap…!

QUINN (*exasperated*). Jesus Christ…!

DUNNE. The shower falls upon me like…? like butterfly kisses and I think of you in your chamber, beneath your shower, madame.

QUINN. And what lucky drops they are…

DUNNE. Oh yes! When one thinks of the useless life of some water. The dark days of toilet water, for example. Water used for nothing more than filling a cistern and pulverising a petrous turd…

QUINN *grabs him, pulls him out of his light and whispers…*

QUINN. Focus on her!!

DUNNE. It's all for her! I'm channelling this poetry through her…! I will not be edited by a lesser scribe!

QUINN. You reason with him, Fitz!

DUNNE. Reason with creation?! I will not be reasoned with!

QUINN. You are not an actor!

DUNNE. Unhand me, sir!

FITZ (*snaps*). For God's sake, Burns, do something!

BURNS *turns to them and raises his bottle.*

BURNS. I am. (*Slight pause.*) I'm escaping.

BURNS *drinks.* FITZ *has an idea. He places a new CD in the stereo.* 'Morning Mood' from Peer Gynt *begins.*

FITZ (*to* QUINN). Can't do any harm.

DUNNE *resumes his attempted courtship, the pastoral music embellishing his already turgid lyricism.*

DUNNE *drops his robe. He's wearing tiger-print Speedos.*

DUNNE. I'm standing, Penelope, on my roughened tiled floor, drying my naked body in God's morning sunshine, the Ionian breeze drying the tear-like droplets from my bristling shoulders.

FITZ. Oh, that's nice, Dunne. Very nice.

DUNNE. A bird? A bird makes me turn to the open window... a blackbird on my sill and what a dainty little fellow with his singing... warming what cockles are left in my arid heart.

QUINN. The more he sings, the more he speaks of you, Penelope.

DUNNE. Is it a message then, Quinn?

QUINN. A message, yes.

DUNNE. A what...?

FITZ. It is a call, Dunne!!

DUNNE. Yes, a siren, I would say, Fitz! For all at once I am under that bird's spell. The singing, it creates a carousel in my mind! It churns within me, rebuilding me, refashioning me, reupholstering an even greater Dunne, more Godly Dunne, more Well-Done Dunne!

QUINN. You step outside with that bird flying above you leading you to her beauty, her grace, Penelope's arms.

DUNNE. Oh yes!

QUINN. The sharp rocks conspire to see you imprisoned in your lonesome cove, that tiny house...

DUNNE. Bastards!

QUINN. ...but you, Dunne, you are a new man! Fashioned by the power of her love!

FITZ. And how the cypress and hyacinth greet him, Quinn.

QUINN. Today like no other day, for they see the man he has become, Fitz.

FITZ (*impressed by* QUINN's *poetry*). Nice.

QUINN. They see the transformation love can have... on even the most... (*He can't help himself.*) annoying of fuckers.

DUNNE. And yet... dear fellow travellers... I have mortal doubts. (*Slight pause.*) How can I even be in Penelope's shadow? How can I taunt myself with the idea of a touch... not so much a touch but even a kind look? She is beyond words, beyond description. Even a master scribe as I am can not conjure up her beauty in tiny letters, in exhausted words.

QUINN *wants to thump him.*

I walk over the parched grass, the lavender alive with a million bees all looking at my new self but sensing my familiar nerves. Their buzzing adds within me layers of doubts... doubts upon doubts and how these doubts round my shoulders and wrinkle my brow and buckle my knees... (*He collapses on the ground.*) till I am bent over on all fours like a wounded hound, wishing away his life, longing to be put asleep eternally, placed in a bucket and pushed out to the calm of the Ionian Sea. (*Slight pause. Whispered.*) I am... nothing to her.

DUNNE *whimpers and sobs a little.*

QUINN *and* FITZ *share a look. They should leave the old ham on the ground but they need to recharge him.*

QUINN. And yet... she calls you.

A pause.

DUNNE (*feigning weakness*). Calls me? Does she, Quinn?

QUINN. The bird again sings... and this time by Penelope's open door. The melody of the bird's voice, of what it means, has you standing again, Dunne. Anxiety falls from your fingertips... and evaporates.

DUNNE. What power I feel.

QUINN (*instructing him*). Well, get up then.

DUNNE *gets his body upright.*

DUNNE. Blood surges through my powerful body, it puffs colour into my cheeks, thickens my hair, fattens my arms, boys! (*Like some primal roar.*) YOU WANT ME! (*Slight pause.*) Each step towards the open door and I stand on shards of your husband's past, Penelope! I crush beneath me his heroics! I claim them as mine!

QUINN. All right, Dunne...

DUNNE. I move quickly through the door! Into your home and your memories of him, Penelope! (*Losing it.*) I take those memories and devour them... (*He devours them.*) and in an instant I am your memories! I am claiming this house for the

27

years of longing… of waiting… for the 'what ifs' and 'maybes'. Do you not recognise my past!?

QUINN. Stop it…!

DUNNE. The man I was, the respect the world showed to me! Do you not see in me… PEDIGREE?!

The red light on the CCTV goes off, PENELOPE *disappears and the camera pivots away from* DUNNE.

This infuriates DUNNE *even more. He turns from the microphone, runs to the ladder and begins to climb it.*

I have given my life to a possibility of love with you…! But you have turned me into this… this notion of a man who BEGS!

FITZ *holds on to* DUNNE's *legs as he tries to get out of the pool.*

I am worthy of this house, of this prize, but you have reduced me, Penelope… to a fat man in SPEEDOS, FOR FUCK'S SAKE!

DUNNE *collapses on the ladder.*

'Morning Mood' continues gently to its end. It seems even more foolish now.

DUNNE *quietly steps back into the pool and* FITZ *helps him back on with his robe.*

BURNS *wanders over to him and hands him his margarita as 'Morning Mood' comes to its natural end.*

BURNS (*whispers to* DUNNE). Love… your… work.

Furious, QUINN *takes* BURNS *firmly by the arm and leads him away from the other two to have a word. They stop and stand facing each other.*

QUINN *suddenly smashes him across the face.*

QUINN. What are you doing?

BURNS. Expressing my dissatisfaction!

QUINN. About what?

BURNS. THIS, QUINN!

QUINN. Get me a drink, Fitz!

BURNS. Oh, I couldn't get Murray's blood off the wall, by the way!

QUINN. Right.

BURNS. You'd think on a tiled surface it'd be easy. Remarkably tricky... and then there's the grouting...!

QUINN. You're not going to help us then?

BURNS. There's no point. We're the talking dead. Now I want to talk about my friend Murray...

QUINN. Go on then...

BURNS. And what happened...

QUINN. Wasn't really a surprise, was it?

BURNS. He was all I had here...

QUINN. You were in love with Murray?

BURNS. I loved him as a friend...

QUINN. You're joking me!

BURNS. It's possible for a platonic love to exist between two men... even in a drained swimming pool, even after all this time living in each other's stink...!

QUINN. Well, if you say it's possible, it might very well be.

BURNS. We were close...!

QUINN. I never saw it.

BURNS. It was the beginning of a friendship!

QUINN. And to be cut short so tragically! My God!

BURNS. You killed him...

QUINN. I thought he slit his own wrists! Didn't he slit his own wrists, Fitz?

FITZ. Like a professional!

BURNS. You spoke him into a corner, scraped away any
possibilities he may have had! We all saw you doing it and
did nothing to stop it! He was my friend, Quinn…!

QUINN. He was competition! Jesus Christ! A 'friend'?! (*Slight
pause*.) I sat around listening to him talking to Penelope and
the words he could use and how he would bring those words
together. I'd go home to that shitty little house by the cove.
I'd go over my new courtship, re-edit, redefine, restructure.
All this time I can feel Murray itching away, yeah. Always the
better sale than me, always the clearer presentation! He was
the best of us, right?

BURNS. She seemed to like him best.

QUINN. Right, so I got into his head, of course I did!

BURNS. I saw.

QUINN. I got close and Murray makes the mistake that we're
friends suddenly. And I see little insecurities in him and we're
speaking the same things… that we're all living this hell and
the gods have forgotten us and that there is no Penelope
even… there's only us in our little houses, us making the
journey up the little path to this empty house, us in the pool
trying to think of new ways to win a love that's un-fucking-
winnable! 'She's not even there, Murray!', I say. 'The gods
are not up there any more! We are being eaten by madness!'
I'm speaking at him so that he has no time to speak himself. I
wear Murray down like an old rag! He's not Murray to me
any more, he's not even human. We share little pleasantries in
the morning but I'm steering his moods, counting his words,
building little corners and placing that little fucker in those
corners! I might have just slit his throat but where's the
sophistication in that, Burns? That's common! You understand
that, right?! We've got a lot of time on our hands down here!
We are all here to win and each second is a game! So let's
play the game! We are all men of business! We bring what we
were in the old world to this place! We are all the same type
of men! Murray would sell his dead granny for a deal. He
would have to find her grave first, 'cause let's face it, he
wouldn't have showed at the funeral. He would buy a spade,
go to that grave, dig her up, crash her out of that coffin, throw

her in the back of his Lexus and sell her decaying, filthy arse because he loved money! We are all like that, Burns!

BURNS. I don't want to be like that any more...

QUINN. You feel some allegiance to me, Fitz and Dunne?

BURNS. To a point, yes...

QUINN. Great! Then you won't have any problems getting onside and helping one of us win Penelope! Now shut the fuck up, get off the drink and get onside! (*Turning to the others*.) So it's me up next, men! The Mighty Quinn! What happened, Dunne... oh Jesus, man...!?

DUNNE. Obviously the day that's in it, Quinn...

QUINN. Right.

DUNNE. Went for something traditional, something that may appeal to her more literary sensibilities but I couldn't control my bile.

QUINN. I find a shit in the morning helps.

DUNNE. I hope I live to see my next movement.

QUINN. And me mine.

DUNNE. Whatever the outcome, whether it's my murderous death or losing Penelope to one of you three, they were my final words of romance, sadly.

QUINN. That is a tragedy.

DUNNE. Had I made it into her house and arms I feel certain that I would have investigated a life in theatre. I have a musicality and subtlety all of my own. How and what I performed just ten minutes ago is a complete mystery to me.

QUINN. It's the mark of a great artist that you found truth in such wonderful delusion.

DUNNE. Thank you, Quinn. That is a consolation.

BURNS *walks back to the back wall. He traces his finger down the bloodstained grouting.*

QUINN. You look a bit tight, Mr Fitz!

FITZ (*trying to read his book*). Feeling a bit tight, Mr Quinn... just trying to stave off images of my barbecued flesh and lose myself in the companionship of some epic poetry.

QUINN. You stay in that happy place, Fitzy!

FITZ. Understood.

QUINN. I've been working on a new pursuit that may very well be my greatest illusion yet! With Dunne having shot his load and Murray dead I'm clearly our best bet today, right, men?

FITZ. Yes, definitely, Quinn.

DUNNE. Absolutely.

QUINN. Burns has got all the passion of a corpse and, with drink taken, is about as useful as a cock in a convent... you, Fitz, let's be honest...

FITZ. Please do.

QUINN. Your seduction has all the skill of a fingerless fool filleting a fish.

FITZ. That's true.

BURNS *quickly goes to the table, grabs the metal bucket from underneath...*

QUINN. What you have in me, gentlemen, is consistency! Prepare yourself for the moment consistency meets innovation...!

BURNS *flings the metal bucket against the wall. Bloody water splatters everywhere.*

A pause. BURNS *calmly walks over to* QUINN. *He stops beside him.*

BURNS. Can I just step into your shit and have a quiet word?

QUINN. Say it now, I'm about to change.

A pause.

BURNS. I am no longer your junior, Quinn. We are all equals as of the moment we had our prophesy.

QUINN. Well, if it makes you happy to think that... fine.

BURNS *takes off his party hat and flings it aside.*

BURNS. Let me say it clearly so you understand the direction of the day and the day's probable outcome.

QUINN. Make it quick.

BURNS. For the short remainder of our lives... you will continue to use your notions of love to entrap this desperate woman. The more you talk, the more you steal the world of any truth. Today I can finally see that clearer than ever. (*Slight pause.*) I have no hopes now but for this one hope, Quinn.

QUINN. Yeah and what's that then, lover?

BURNS. That after squeezing the life out of Fitz's heart... her husband turns to you... bends you over... reaches up your arsehole and rips out your poisonous brain. I want to live to see that.

BURNS *raises his bottle of spirits and makes a toast.*

Let real love speak!

BURNS *drinks.*

Suddenly the red light appears on the camera, the follow spot beams down on FITZ *and* PENELOPE *is seen watching her television.*

FITZ *is 'on'.*

FITZ. Oh, crap....

DUNNE (*loud whisper*). Quinn!?

QUINN *turns and sees* FITZ *is 'on'.*

QUINN. Oh, for FUCK'S SAKE!

FITZ *places his book down on his pool lounger, walks to the microphone, stares up at the camera and begins very badly.*

FITZ (*terrified*). Now that I'm... is it not...? the... how can I in words...? there are... they say at least... as I would... unconditionally... speaking...

QUINN *and* DUNNE *go to the trestle table and fix themselves some drinks as* FITZ *crumbles in front of them.*

33

…and often should be… listen with an open… Penelope. Am I not…? I concur with previous… with an honest… setting aside all… between elements of… (*Pleads*.) Quinn, please help me!

QUINN *turns and looks at him but offers him nothing. He walks behind the standing screen in the corner.*

Dunne?

DUNNE *turns away from him.*

FITZ *knows he's alone. He tries to drag up anything from his drug-addled mind.*

And if I could… and if it was possible I would. (*Slight pause*.) Because back inside here… (*Slight pause*.) back in the place where no one can see… (*Slight pause*.) there's little pauses, little pools of nothing. (*Slight pause*.) And I can be there. Deeper than the deepest sleep with no thoughts, no itchy wants throwing me into the next thing, the next page, the next piece of noise. I can be there. (*Slight pause*.) And maybe I can stretch this nothing further and is it possible to take these pools of nothing and shape a new world? Is there anyone who can stop me other than me? So I go about constructing a house out of this material, place this nothing house on a nothing island, by a nothing cove, in a nothing atmosphere. Place my glorious nothing self in this nothing house and bask in nothing. In the real world people are shunted from scene to scene, packed with half-knowledge, half-truths. What a world they've made! And where does truth exist and how does anyone breathe in that world? How do doors open and how do people leave their houses? And what makes them want to talk or need to listen or feel obliged to experience things? And how is it possible that they can fall asleep and rise again and fill a day and mark that day and sleep and wake and live in that world? It's called living apparently. How horrible that world is! But I'm in my house of nothing and high in the distance I can see those people on Earth 'living'. I look at them indifferently, without conscience, without pity, it means nothing to me because I am a world onto myself now. Here alone, a body, a house, an atmosphere, wonderfully indifferent, blissfully uncaring. My body pumps and breathes independently and I've ordered my thoughts so that now I have few thoughts or perhaps I've no thoughts any more. When I think of my youth and what I have sold and what I have gathered and what I have lost and what I have gained and what little effect my youth has had on any existence! I am a blemish, Penelope! A tampering twit who's used life, tossed it aside, rolled it in my fingertips, placed it in an ashtray, pushed it down the back of the couch, flicked life across a tabletop! But I will forget my past, forget the real world, sit in my nothingness and begin with a new idea... an idea... of... (*He clears his head and the word forms.*) you.

FITZ *takes a breath.*

PENELOPE *is seen standing up from her seat. From behind the curtain she looks towards the pool.*

BURNS *and* DUNNE *don't see this as* QUINN *remains behind the screen, changing.*

I put aside all the stories I've ever made about you, all the dreams I've ever dreamt, of which there are millions... what use are they when they are nothing of you. But still I must begin somewhere with some idea of you. And I do. (*Slight pause.*) The idea arrives not as a physical thing or a smell or a scent of any sort but this tiny feeling. And it begins in my stomach because it's stomach-felt and it bleeds into my heart and it holds the heartbeat.

PENELOPE *raises the curtain and looks down on* FITZ. *For the first time we see her true beauty. She hasn't aged. She is a woman in her early twenties.*

And it grows in an unchartered place this feeling but in a world of nothing it is the only thing I have and I help it grow inside me and I allow it to claim my small world, my whole self. It takes everything that I am, that I want to be and it will lead me to you in time.

QUINN *appears dressed in a black morning suit. He's staring at* PENELOPE *and the connection* FITZ *has made with her. He's panicked.*

And lead me through the tedious detail of the island that I have spoken and dreamt into extinction. Lead me to opening my door, to taking a chance. I long for love! For this all-consuming love as you must long for it. And in truth it is nothing of you, the physical you but it is everything that this feeling is! Do you understand this?!

QUINN *is looking for something. He finds* FITZ*'s beloved book and walks over to the barbecue. He places it on the grill.* FITZ *doesn't yet see this as he's hypnotised by* PENELOPE.

How it holds my heart and how I know after all these years of longing for your husband it must hold yours too...! Can you see in me a possibility? A possibility to keep love faceless... and just love the love itself!?

QUINN *walks back to the trestle table, grabs the blowtorch, fires it up and walks back to the barbecue.*

We are two souls longing for a love to grow from a glorious nothing! Throw open your door and let us start with care...!

QUINN *pulverises Homer.* FITZ *suddenly sees what he's doing, breaks and races to the barbecue.*

MY GOD, NO! NOOOOOOOO!

He pushes QUINN *aside and rescues his book.* FITZ *falls to his knees and frantically puts out the flames.*

The curtain drops on PENELOPE, *the camera switches off and she disappears.*

QUINN *turns off the blowtorch and walks back to the trestle table and puts the blowtorch back.*

BURNS *suddenly spits a mouthful of whiskey into* QUINN*'s face.* QUINN *grabs at his eyes as* BURNS *punches him in the head.*

The two begin to fight badly.

DUNNE *walks up to a sobbing* FITZ *as he tries to put the book back together.*

DUNNE (*to* FITZ). Just the one note?

FITZ. What is it?

DUNNE. More energy. And don't be afraid of the gag.

A slight pause.

FITZ. That's two notes.

DUNNE. Second one was free.

BURNS, *sitting on* QUINN*'s chest, screams in anger/frustration.*

He's holding a Peperami above his head like he's going to stab QUINN.

QUINN. Is that a Peperami in your hand?

BURNS. Probably. Maybe. Is it? (*He looks.*) Yes.

BURNS *holds it to* QUINN*'s throat.*

QUINN. So what do you plan to do?

BURNS. I don't know yet.

QUINN. It won't kill me if that's what you have in mind.

BURNS. I'm compiling a list of possible ways to murder you, force-feeding you reconstituted meats I'll happily add to that list.

QUINN. That will take a lot of patience.

BURNS. I have a lot of patience.

QUINN. Patience you might have but Peperami and time you don't. He's coming!

BURNS *gets off him.*

He's coming, men! He's coming!

BURNS. All this time she's never opened her curtain and shown herself but it was Fitz's words and for the first time honest words…!

FITZ. And it's impossible to say where this honesty has come from!

DUNNE (*grandly*). From the tiniest light within your darkened soul.

FITZ (*in awe*). Holy God!

DUNNE. Of course she may have been stunned by my poetry earlier…

QUINN (*to* DUNNE). Oh, shut up!

BURNS. We had a chance, Quinn!

DUNNE. ...woke from her reverie and searched out my melodious tones! She did meet my eye just then, Fitz! Fleetingly it was but we stared into each other's hearts at that very moment. In hers I saw devotion and can you guess what she saw in mine?

FITZ. Stenosis.

DUNNE. Yes, obviously... but seeping from my thick ventricles she saw... 'honour'.

BURNS. Has honour ever lived here, Dunne?

DUNNE. What are you talking about!? We are men of integrity, Burns! I shit honour!

BURNS. But will you ever return to reality?

DUNNE. What reality?

BURNS. *A* reality!

DUNNE. I am in one!

BURNS. A reality closer to what the people of the world may ACTUALLY RECOGNISE! I mean, look at us!

DUNNE. How dare you bring the world into this! I have spent a lifetime escaping the world! What the fuck has the world ever given to me?!

FITZ. Given you nothing but you've taken enough!

DUNNE. I most certainly did! And I am owed Penelope's love!

BURNS. But your words have meant nothing to her! She's an object to you, an ending, another deal! Look how she reacted to Fitz just now. He was speaking not to trick her and win his way into her house but he spoke with a simple truth from his heart!

FITZ. Faced by my immediate barbecuing I have developed a goodness! Holy shit!

QUINN. It had nothing to do with your words! Her husband is close, her heart can feel it… now more than any other time she is open to seduction!

FITZ. But it might have been with me, Quinn!

QUINN. And how could I live with myself knowing that you'd be in that house?!

BURNS. But we would have been saved from a terrible death!

QUINN. And beaten by him! Alive but knowing that she was stolen from me! This is Fitz we're talking about here! Look at him, for fuck's sake! No offence, Fitz…

FITZ. We're past that…

QUINN. …but this is a decaying man, an incontinent near-imbecile, a man whose manhood has shrivelled to boyhood… could you happily deposit this geriatric at her door!? Of course you couldn't!

BURNS. So the fight continues.

QUINN. Of course the fight continues!

DUNNE. And we're opposition again?

BURNS. We always will be.

FITZ. This working together? This company!

QUINN. An aberration!

FITZ. This trust?

QUINN. A deviation!

FITZ. Excellent!

DUNNE. Then can I add that Fitz is also a junkie!

FITZ. I step into that madness with all the happy expectation of a plankton drifting the oceans of the world, Dunne. You are a jealous bastard!

DUNNE. And you are a terrible bastard!

FITZ. You have all the erudition of a pig defecating his day's feed!

DUNNE. Your brain has the consistency and the imagination of that pig defecation!

FITZ. Shithead!

DUNNE. You are the shithead, thou vicious mole of nature!

> DUNNE *flings a Twiglet into* FITZ's *face.* FITZ *grabs a half-eaten sandwich and throws it at* DUNNE's *face.* DUNNE *grabs his Martini and throws it in* FITZ's *face.* FITZ *grabs his gin and tonic and throws it in* DUNNE's *face.* DUNNE *slaps* FITZ *across the face.* FITZ *punches* DUNNE *in the stomach.*

> Enough! (*Drops to his knees.*) Enough!

BURNS. Not one of us is worthy of her, Quinn!

QUINN. I am worthy of her!

BURNS. Years ago as a healthier man you might have imagined it. But you saw her beauty just now! All these years and she is the same woman and even if she was seduced by your lies how could you even think of her taken in by your looks and that abomination you call hair!

FITZ. His hair's his best feature!

BURNS. His hair is fake!

FITZ. A wig?!

BURNS. It's dyed!

FITZ. A dyed wig?

BURNS. Just dyed.

FITZ. My God, really?!

DUNNE. No man is worthy of Penelope's affection when he wears his mock virility on his head! You fraudulent follicle-er!

BURNS. Stop talking like that!!

QUINN. What makes me worthy is that I'm stronger than you, Burns. Stronger than the lot of ya! I was born strong!

FITZ. Your melanin wasn't!

QUINN. I see that I'm losing her and straight away I'm thinking… I'll take death… whatever he carves me into… I'll take it over the humiliation of losing out to Fitz! That's how strong I am! Annihilation versus the shame…!

BURNS. So what have you won just now?

QUINN. Control, you idiot! You know that!

BURNS. How can you talk about love when you don't even have compassion for your own life? Me… I cared for someone!

QUINN. For Murray?

BURNS. It was the start of a bond!

QUINN. Did you feel some brotherhood with this man?

BURNS. Yes.

QUINN. Why?

BURNS. Why did I like him?

QUINN. Why did you feel you should like him?

BURNS. I wasn't consciously thinking, 'I should like this man…'

QUINN. Weren't you?

BURNS. He was my friend!

QUINN. What did you want from him?

BURNS. Nothing!

QUINN. Something.

BURNS. Companionship, trust…

QUINN. I know what you are and what men do… and what we don't do is 'trust'!

FITZ. It's true.

QUINN. You're sat opposite Murray and you're telling me you're not working out ways of beating this fucker!?

BURNS. I'm not!

QUINN. It's all just innocent chit-chat, little bits of banter that brings you and Murray closer together.

BURNS. It's called friendship, Quinn!

QUINN. You would smash Murray into the ground! What makes me worthy, Burns, is that I'll say it out straight! I will crush Murray, I will turn on each one of you because I must! You stand in my way and I'll chop you down because that is what I was, what I still am! How many men were here? At the beginning? How many, Fitz?

FITZ. A hundred or so.

QUINN. A hundred men living on this rock all fighting for her love, yeah. The weaker ones are out by that first summer. Years pass and more are driven mad, remember! We're queuing up to seduce Penelope but nothing happens and heads drop. Men are toppin' themselves every other night. Did ya care about any of those men?!

BURNS. No.

QUINN. Of course you didn't! You hated them like I did, right?!

BURNS. I hated some…

QUINN. And now you've all of a sudden got yourself some humanity?! Does it make you feel better that you can feel for another person? Makes you more whole, more human than me?

BURNS. Well, yes it does!

QUINN. You're a liar…

BURNS. I know what I'm feeling! The way we have lived… these shameless lives we've lived here…!

QUINN. We are the last men! We've survived here because we've understood our nature, Burns. Men go out into the world, begin a day with all notion of honesty, of law, of community. But you think that notion lasts!?

BURNS. If we tried to make it last…!

QUINN. What if our waking impulse is to feel at ease with life, yeah? Like life nurtures you and in return you give life back

kindness, respect? That you allow life's annoying little
mishaps, you take them on the chin, you meet badness with a
little smile, a shrug of the shoulders. Some idiot's talking too
loud or not making sense or plainly lying through his teeth but
you allow his loudness, his idiocy, his conniving thieving
ways because today, Burns, today you are in harmony with
life! You are a virtuous man, a compassionate human being, a
liberal hugger of humanity! For the brand new Burns, this is
good, right?! This is how the gods would have planned it too.
A planet of the merciful! Is that idea compelling to you,
Burns?

BURNS. Yes!

QUINN. This new-found honesty that's suddenly lit up in your
black... your blacker-than-black fucking soul, Burns... well,
this new you must be banging his tambourine at this new
world order, marching towards this glorious utopia...

FITZ. It does sound nice...

QUINN. It's a rainbow, is what it is, Fitz, and he knows it! We
eat life! We annihilate every single thing that doesn't comply
to our tastes, to our sense of good, our idea of beauty. Each
second of the day is a challenge to control, to win, to shape,
right, Burns?! Each little sight you see is there to be turned
sour, yeah. Each person we meet is there to be beaten down
and knocked into place. It's subtle at first, otherwise it's all a
bit aggressive and a little too obvious for us men of the world.
But idle chit-chat is there to be won, friendships are there to
be used, love is a fucking weapon. This impulse, boys, this is
what shapes life! This is our muscle! This is how we are the
last four men standing! I'm working on reducing Murray, the
great Murray, to some gibbering wreck, yeah! I'm wearing
him down, placing that knife in his hand, placing that knife on
his wrists and not one of you stepped in! Not you either,
Burns! And why's that? 'Cause you wanted to see 'your
friend' dead! I'm right, amn't I?!

BURNS. No...

QUINN. 'Cause you're one step closer to Penelope that way! In
your stomach you have some tiny illusion to do good but
every history of you, every fibre of Burns is carved from hate!

Hate is our friend! Hate evolves our spirit, our dreams, our society! We came to this island to win the island and we'll use what we can to win her, to win our freedom, to win power! What do you know about love, Burns!? With whatever means you must triumph and crush... that is your one fucking belief! Without keeping that alive, what has your life been, man? Nothing!

Silence as BURNS, DUNNE *and* FITZ *stare at the all-powerful* QUINN.

QUINN *picks up the party hat and places it back on* BURNS*'s head.*

Now unless I'm mistaken... it's me up next, right? Same moves as before with some added illusion. Do you understand me?

BURNS *remains silent.* QUINN *goes for a softer approach.*

I won't be stopped. 'Less you toe the line I swear to God I'll cut you up like a crazed Boy Scout butchering a chicken. Can you imagine that?

BURNS. Yes.

QUINN. Good boy.

BURNS *stands hanging his head as* QUINN, FITZ *and* DUNNE *look at him.*

QUINN *gets the large helium-filled heart balloon and places it on the barbecue.*

His boat's close... I can feel it. He can see the island. (*Slight pause.*) Now get behind me, men.

QUINN *walks behind the standing screen.*

BURNS, DUNNE *and* FITZ *stand beaten. They're finished.*

FITZ *stares longingly into the empty tablet container. He turns it over and fails to shake anything out.*

FITZ. There's nothing to fight for. I always imagined my dying would be like this. I fought all my life and now I'm leaving with complete indifference. I have left... nothing.

BURNS. We're dead men.

A long pause. Then…

DUNNE. Gravity should at least take some of the blame.
(*Pause*.) People can't help making things, nature decays and
rebuilds in the blink of an eye… and the surface of the
planet's so busy. These days it's difficult to remember where
I've come from. I might close my eyes and shards of past lie
next to bits of half-memories and it's impossible to tell
whether I've featured in my life and what needs saving from
it and what needs saving now. (*Slight pause*.) I turn off gravity
and stand about and watch the oceans tumble into space,
watch the animals and fish fall away from the Earth, see the
little birds blown into nothing like dust. People cling to
themselves and onto their machines and soon space is littered
with centuries of debris. Up there and humanity doesn't
amount to a great deal but down here on Earth it's very quiet
with just me lying on my back on the grass. (*Slight pause*.)
Lying in our garden somewhere between awake and asleep
with the sun on my face. I could easily fall into sleep but the
inside of the house is calling me. I stand up and see my
reflection in the kitchen window and I'm looking at my ten-
year-old self. I look down on my young hands and walk my
ten-year-old body towards the inside. Already in the walk my
heart feels lighter, the colours saturating around me. There's
no burden of the past here, no bad memories to taint, no
memories at all to colour, no future to ponder or tease… just
my ten-year-old self walking with the warm sun for company
and the expectation of a good thing. I enter the house. And it's
still inside the house. The temperature drops a little and cools
my brow. I walk to the kitchen and stop at the door. (*Slight
pause*.) I'm watching my mother taking a glass from the shelf
and filling it with milk. She opens the press and takes out a
packet of biscuits and places two on a little saucer. I know it's
my milk and biscuits. She feels me watching her and turns
around then. And I smile at her from the door. The scene
suspended then in its own space with no past or future, no
hidden story itching badly underneath, just me with a smile on
my mouth and the beginnings of a smile in my mother's eyes.
I let my heart lead me now and I move and go to her and
throw my arms about her. I bury my head in that big chest of
hers and she folds around me and kisses the top of my head.
Her breathing me up, me breathing her in and both wanting to

disappear into what...? into our love. (*Slight pause*.) Gravity has done away with people and their things and me and mother begin a new life. From our little kitchen this love breathes out into the world. (*Slight pause*.) And what happiness.

This quiet revolution in DUNNE *has stirred* FITZ *and* BURNS.

Suddenly the door into PENELOPE*'s house opens. She steps down and looks down at the three men.*

She walks around the side of the pool, stops and stands just above the CCTV camera looking at them. There's an intensity to her. She's waiting. Something is going to happen.

FITZ (*aside*). We need to bury our corruption and let love survive this pool. Say it could be done, Burns.

BURNS (*aside*). We have been terrible men... and even now each of us knows what terrible thing must happen next. (*Slight pause*.) But I swear to whatever ounce of goodness I may still have inside me, boys... (*Slight pause*.) If we fight to let love win, even in death us three would be free.

DUNNE. Do it, so.

BURNS *presses the stereo and 'Spanish Flea' by Herb Alpert and the Tijuana Brass blasts out.*

BURNS, DUNNE *and* FITZ *look back at the screen.*

The French tricolour unravels over the standing screen as QUINN *bursts 'onstage' costumed as a tiny Napoleon Bonaparte adorned with an oversized bicorn naval hat and naval uniform.* QUINN *immediately sees* PENELOPE. *This gives him immense confidence. He begins to play out a short scenario where 'Napoleon' slaughters imaginary enemies with his sword. He takes out a map and looks over the expanding French Empire. He turns it over and with a quill he mimes writing a love letter. He kisses it, folds it a few times and hands it to* BURNS. BURNS, *like the dutiful assistant, unravels it and magically it has turned into a paper dove.*

QUINN *disappears momentarily behind the screen as* BURNS *'flies' the dove across the stage.*

QUINN *reappears as a weeping Josephine de Beauharnais,
wife of Napoleon. Only now do we realise we're watching a
very accomplished quick-change cabaret routine with illusion.*
QUINN *is dressed in a long silk dress, a brown wig curled
around his powdered face. 'Josephine' sees the dove and tries
to catch it but it is always out of reach. She pulls a pistol from
her handbag and shoots it. The dove falls into her hands.
Josephine opens the dove and reads the love letter from
Napoleon. She breaks into a smile showing her rotting teeth
and disappears behind the screen.*

*'Spanish Flea' cuts into 'A Taste of Honey' by Herb Alpert
and the Tijuana Brass.*

BURNS *holds out a walking cane for* QUINN *as he
reappears dressed as Rhett Butler from* Gone with the Wind.
*He takes the cane and swaggers about all Clark Gable-style,
removing the French tricolour which suddenly becomes the
American Confederate flag. In his hands the cane becomes a
large bunch of flowers. He throws the flowers to* BURNS *who
catches them.*

QUINN *disappears behind the screen once more.*

*He suddenly reappears as Scarlett O'Hara in bloomers,
corset and bonnet. 'She' snaps the flowers out of* BURNS*'s
hands and smells them. The flowers wither in her hands. She
falls to her knees, cries and waves a fist at God for mercy.*

QUINN *goes back behind the screen and immediately
appears above the screen as Shakespeare's Juliet at her
balcony.*

*'A Taste of Honey' cuts into 'I'll Never Fall in Love Again' by
Herb Alpert and the Tijuana Brass.*

*Another drape falls over the screen showing flowers on a
garden trellis. A tiny sparrow lands on 'Juliet's' hand. Juliet
pets it and suddenly it becomes a vial of poison. She throws it
in the air and* BURNS *just about catches it.* QUINN *vanishes
as* BURNS *places the vial on a tiny silk pillow.*

QUINN *reappears as the distressed Romeo. 'Romeo' sees the
vial of poison, cries and lays his head down on the pillow. He
drinks his own poison and 'dies'.* BURNS *places the standing*

47

screen drape over Romeo's body. From underneath, Juliet suddenly reappears, distraught. She takes Romeo's dagger and stabs herself. She 'dies'.

BURNS *grabs* QUINN'*s feet and drags him back towards the screen.*

He nods at FITZ *and* DUNNE *to get ready to attack.*

'I'll Never Fall in Love Again' cuts into 'America' by Herb Alpert and the Tijuana Brass.

BURNS *and* QUINN *are back behind the screen.* FITZ *and* DUNNE *rifle through the debris on the table, looking for something to kill* QUINN *with. They find various useless implements and stab the air with a corkscrew, snooker cue, a tennis racket, etc. Finally* DUNNE *finds a knife.* FITZ *takes it off him.* FITZ *wants to do it. They face the screen.*

QUINN *reappears costumed as Jackie Kennedy with* BURNS *costumed as JFK. They wave from their car when suddenly 'JFK's' head explodes. 'Jackie' cradles the dead body like* La Pietà *and cries.*

QUINN *then stands and takes off his Jackie costume. Underneath he is dressed as Eros the Greek God of Love with wonderful wings.*

'America' cuts into 'Zorba the Greek' by Herb Alpert and the Tijuana Brass.

QUINN *takes the heart balloon, cuts its string and holds it out to* PENELOPE. *He lets go of it and it floats up and into* PENELOPE'*s hands.*

PENELOPE *is about to smile.*

Suddenly FITZ *is over fast. He stabs* QUINN *on the side.*

QUINN *grabs at the wound and turns to* FITZ.

QUINN (*gasping*). You whittled a penny whistle...? You fucking liar!

DUNNE *grabs* QUINN *and holds his arms back.*

DUNNE (*shouts*). Finish him!

FITZ *stabs him again.* BURNS *is over fast, takes the knife and drives it into* QUINN*'s stomach.*

BURNS *pulls the knife out and* QUINN *falls to the ground, the balloon exploding in* PENELOPE*'s hands.*

PENELOPE *turns away fast to re-enter the house but...*

BURNS (*calls*). Wait!!

FITZ *slams off the stereo.* PENELOPE *stops but doesn't yet turn around.*

I'm trying to be good...

Like DUNNE *and* FITZ, BURNS *is covered in* QUINN*'s blood.*

PENELOPE *has remained still.* BURNS *needs to speak but has drawn a blank.*

A pause. Then quietly to start...

Outside of here there must be a world. (*Slight pause.*) There's other places and colours and there must be cities and towns and villages with people, right? Stories must clash about and finish abruptly or start afresh and live for moments or maybe days even. And these stories must be shapeless and free and twist into new directions and possibilities. And the people who live these stories must have frustrations and worries... they must be annoyed by these stories and have anxieties about the outcome of these stories or have excitement about the stories' possible endings... I don't know. And people move about from one story to the next, from a moment's conversation to a whole life's dialogue, maybe. And outside they have this and people can get to live in this shapeless incredible... adventure. (*Slight pause.*) And it's not just words 'cause mostly life outside is lived by just looking and being in the world. And a corner is turned and a new world opens up and you look down and about and marvel that men have shaped homes from water and dust. Towns disappear into countryside and then into sea and sea into new lands and people get to live a life where possibility, where freedom is brought to life by the simplicity of waking up and sitting up in bed and just being in the world. Can you imagine that life?

(*Slight pause*.) But the brain wakes in the morning and so drunk it is by digesting the world that it wants for order. And what the brain wants the brain gets. Rules are placed on stories, talk is a veil for lies and people carry around little pedestals of differing sizes and half-talk to each other and lie to themselves and others that they are part of a community, part of a civilisation probably. But it needn't be like that, Penelope! It shouldn't be that way! And what if people could open their eyes and sit up in bed like the very first time and just be in the world and let their hearts rule? (*Slight pause*.) Today felt closest to that day. (*Slight pause*.) I woke at the moment I wake every morning, stared at the ceiling I've stared at a thousand times, rolled over in bed and looked out on the Ionian Sea sitting there like some picture postcard. Already each second, each breath, each thing I see feels brand new. It's like my heart has been clicked on and the everyday is brighter suddenly. Things that have sat about lumpen, things that have imprisoned me in their dreariness and routine are now alive. And it's Murray, you see. It didn't seem possible for trust to exist on this island, for friendship to form, but we're talking without lies, we're speaking of other things other than this game we're playing. And if I have a liking and love for this one person perhaps I have the capacity to love other things. I wake with that feeling and my heart is putting it into practice and the world unfolds in front of me brand new and there is such a thing as freedom in this world and only my lack of courage will stop me from breaking out of this shit life I've made for myself here. I take these thoughts to the pool and see Murray's body drained of blood, his spirit escaped but his body slumped there and mocking any notions of a new life that I've brought here this morning! Fuck it! Fuck!

His eyes fill with tears. He stares over at QUINN*'s body. A long pause*.

And still… I won't be beaten by what I've helped to make. (*Slight pause*.) I can't let love die. (*Pause*.) I look up from the pool at the world high above me. (*Slight pause*.) And the Earth spins around with brilliant indifference, us stuck down here, time decaying us and us staring back at fate and grimacing a little. Only love can save us. And I watch that world turning above me and I will and pray for it to happen.

(*Pause.*) It rains. (*Slight pause.*) Like little lights they fall out of the grey towards the pool and maybe I'm lucky enough to catch a drop in my hand. More drops fall. (*Pause.*) And it's hope falling… and freedom… and trust… and goodness… and good dreams… and possible loves… and promise… and real care… and happiness… and sun… and affection… and friendship… and Murray… and tenderness… and love. Of course, love. The world above evaporates in its own darkness and the pool is filling with all this good rain… and it holds now all that is possible, all that will be good, Penelope. (*Slight pause.*) Your beginning… is now.

A pause. PENELOPE *slowly turns and looks down at* BURNS, FITZ *and* DUNNE, *as tears fill her eyes.*

Love is saved.

Suddenly the barbecue goes up in flames. As their dream predicted, it begins from its legs and quickly spreads to the rest of the frame and the grill.

It is a beautiful red/orange fire and BURNS, FITZ *and* DUNNE *stare over at it and into their death.*

They are ready for the end.

The fire rages for one whole minute. PENELOPE *turns and looks offstage and into her new future…*

Blackout.

The End.

51

A Nick Hern Book

Penelope first published in Great Britain in 2010 as a paperback original by Nick Hern Books Limited, 14 Larden Road, London W3 7ST, in association with Druid Theatre Company

Penelope copyright © 2010 Enda Walsh

Enda Walsh has asserted his moral right to be identified as the author of this work

Cover image: Sarah Jones
Cover design: Ned Hoste, 2H

Typeset by Nick Hern Books, London
Printed in Great Britain by CPI Bookmarque, Croydon, Surrey

A CIP catalogue record for this book is available from the British Library

ISBN 978 1 84842 115 8

Mixed Sources
Product group from well-managed forests and other controlled sources
www.fsc.org   Cert no. TT-COC-002227
© 1996 Forest Stewardship Council